INTERFAC

THE BOOK AND DISK THAT WORK TOGETHER

# AZTECS

TWO CAN™

**Created and published by**
**Two-Can Publishing Ltd**
**346 Old Street**
**London**
**EC1V 9NQ**

*Disk*
Creative Director: Jason Page
Programming Director: Paul Steven
Art Director: Sarah Evans
Designer: James Evans
Editor: Lyndall Thomas
Programmer: Colette McFadden
Consultant: Elizabeth Baquedano
Illustrators: James Jarvis, Jeffrey Lewis,
Jon Stuart, Carlo Tartaglia
Production Director: Lorraine Estelle
Production Assistant: Bob Bridle
Project Manager: Joya Bart-Plange

*Book*
Creative Director: Jason Page
Editor: Lyndall Thomas
Designer: Michele Egar
Consultant: Penny Bateman
Production Director: Lorraine Estelle
Production Assistant: Bob Bridle
Project Manager: Joya Bart-Plange



MAC ISBN 1-85434-506-0
PC ISBN 1-85434-502-8
CD ISBN 1-85434-510-9

Dewey Decimal Classification 972

2 4 6 8 10 9 7 5 3 1

A catalogue record for this book is available from the British Library

Printed in Hong Kong by Wing King Tong

Photographic Credits: Werner Forman: front cover, pp12-16, pp18-19, p20 c, p21, p22, pp 24-25, p26, p 34 cl, p47; Toby Maudsley: p19 b, p20 tr; Ronald Sheridan: p12 bl, p17, p34 tr
Illustrations: Harry Clow: pp10-11, p13, p17, p18, pp20-21, pp22-23, p24, p27, p28, p48; Maxine Hamil: pp29-33; Linden Artists: p8, p9, p35

# INTERFACT

## THE BOOK AND DISK THAT WORK TOGETHER

**INTERFACT** will have you hooked in minutes – and that's a fact!

- **The disk is packed with interactive activities, puzzles, quizzes and games that are fun to do and packed with interesting facts.**

Answer as many quiz questions as you can to win balls to use on the tlachtli court.

Read up on what the Aztecs ate, then do some cooking of your own!

- **Open the book and discover more fascinating information highlighted with lots of full-colour illustrations and photographs.**

- To get the most out of **INTERFACT**, use the book and disk together. Look out for the special signs, called Disk Links and Bookmarks. To find out more, turn to page 43.

**BOOKMARK**

**DISK LINK**
**Have a go at an ancient Aztec board game on screen when you PLAY PATOLLI!**

Once you've clicked on to **INTERFACT**, you'll never look back.

**LOAD UP!**
**Go to page 40 to find out how to load your disk and click into action.**

# What's on the disk

## HELP SCREEN

Learn how to use the disk in no time at all.

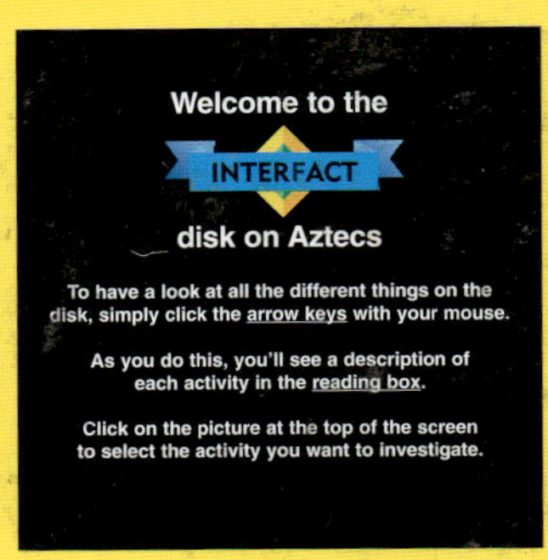


Get to grips with the controls and find out how to use:

- arrow keys
- reading boxes
- 'hot' words

## TIME WARP

Take a trip through time and learn about ancient Mexico.

Discover how the Aztec civilisation began. Learn about the leaders who made the Aztec Empire powerful, then find out how Aztec life was destroyed by the Spanish invasion.

## TLACHTLI CHALLENGE

Get ready to play the sacred Aztec ball game!

Answer quiz questions about the Aztecs and earn balls to use on the tlachtli court. Shoot for the hoop and see how many points you can score.

## AZTEC EXPLORER

Take a scenic tour through the ancient Aztec lands!

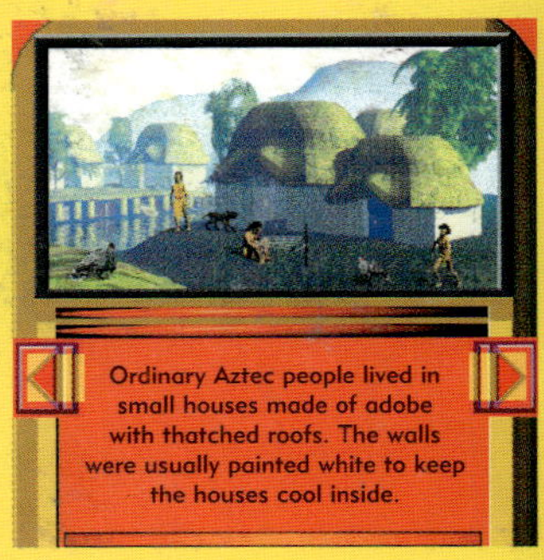


Explore Tenochtitlan, the mighty city at the centre of the Aztec Empire! Take a close-up look at an Aztec farm, or get the inside story on the temple precinct.

## THE GREAT SPEAKER

Get the answers to all your questions about the Aztecs.

**If there is something you want to know about the Aztecs, just ask the Great Speaker. He will answer questions from the crowd and will tell you all about life in Aztec times.**

## FOR SALE

Investigate the amazing Aztec market at Tlatelolco.

**See if you can work out who is who in this busy market scene. Once you've got all the name tags in the right position, go exploring with your mouse and find out what's going on.**

## SURVIVAL ADVENTURE

Put yourself to the test in an interactive adventure story.

**Would you like to live in Aztec times? Travel back through history and find out! You'll need to use all your knowledge of the Aztecs to survive.**

## PLAY PATOLLI

Learn how to play a traditional Aztec game.

**Challenge a friend to a game of patolli – the Aztecs' favourite board game. Place your bets, throw the beans and decide how to make your move!**

# What's in the book

*All words in the text that appear in **bold** can be found in the glossary*

▶ Turquoise serpent of the rain god, Tlaloc
▶ Turquoise mask of Quetzalcoatl
▶ Stone carving of the legendary Tenochtitlan eagle
Atlantic Ocean
ANAHUAC
Teotihuacan
Tenochtitlan
Veracruz
Gulf of Mexico
Tabasco
Pacific Ocean
Lake Texcoco
▶ Temple at Tajin

# The Aztec world

Nearly 500 years ago, a group of people known as the Aztecs ruled over the region we now call Mexico. They called their land **Anahuac**, which means *the land on the edge of the waters*.

The Aztecs were powerful warriors. They built a huge **empire** by attacking and conquering neighbouring peoples.

**▼ There was a busy marketplace in every Aztec town.**

# Tenochtitlan

The capital of the Aztec Empire was called Tenochtitlan. It was built in the middle of a large lake on a **plateau** high up in the mountains.

Tenochtitlan had a population of up to 300,000 people. This made it one of the largest cities in the world at that time.

Tenochtitlan was divided into four districts. The different parts of the city were connected by canals. The most important area was the temple precinct (shown below). Ordinary people lived in neighbourhoods around the centre of the city or in towns on the edge of the lake.

**▼ Many canals ran through the city. The Aztecs did not have horses or vehicles with wheels. They carried everything by boat or on their backs.**

▼ In the middle of Tenochtitlan was the temple precinct. This was where the Aztecs worshipped their gods and performed human **sacrifices**. The largest temple was around 90 m tall and there were more than 100 steps leading up to the top.

**DISK LINK**
Would you like a closer look at Tenochtitlan? Then take a ride in the AZTEC EXPLORER.

▼ Tenochtitlan was built on an island in Lake Texcoco. The land here was damp and marshy.

◀ In Tenochtitlan, many of the canals were joined to the shore by **causeways** built from rock and earth. These had bridges in them that could be destroyed so that attackers could not enter the city.

# Rulers

The Aztec ruler was known as Huey Tlatoani, meaning ***Great Speaker***. He was elected by a council made up of the leaders of the most important Aztec families, or **calpullis**.

The Great Speaker had advisers who helped him to rule. The most important of these advisers was called the Snake Woman – even though he was a man!

It was the Great Speaker's duty to lead the Aztec army into battle. The Aztecs were constantly at war with their neighbours because they needed prisoners to sacrifice to the gods. The lands that were conquered were expected to pay a **tribute** to the Aztecs.

**DISK LINK**
**Would you like to meet an Aztec leader? Then here's your chance! Take a look at THE GREAT SPEAKER.**

▼ **This carved stone box shows a Great Speaker.**

▼ Montezuma II wore this huge and elaborate feather headdress at ceremonies and processions.

## Important leaders

**ITZCOATL** became Great Speaker in 1426. Under his rule, the territory of the Aztec Empire was expanded.

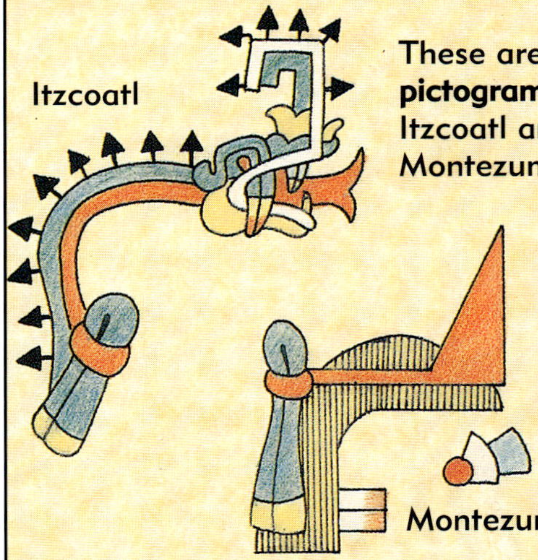


These are **pictograms** of Itzcoatl and Montezuma II.

**MONTEZUMA II** became Great Speaker in 1502 and was leader when the Aztecs were defeated by Spanish explorers (see page 28).

▼ The Great Speaker was very important. Many people believed that the gods had given him special powers.

# Religion

Religion influenced every part of Aztec life. There were gods for different parts of the natural world and for human activities. The Aztecs believed that the gods decided their fate and that priests could predict future events. The gods were linked by a complicated set of **myths** and legends.

The Aztecs developed different types of calendars. The religious calendar had 260 days in a year. There was also a solar calendar that had 365 days in a year, just like ours. The solar year had 18 months, each with 20 days, plus five extra days.

## The fifth sun

The Aztecs believed that they lived in the time of the fifth sun. According to Aztec legend, four earlier suns had been destroyed. The first was destroyed by jaguars, the second by hurricanes, the third by fire and the fourth by floods. They believed that the fifth sun would be destroyed by a huge earthquake.

**▶ This is the Aztec calendar stone. At the centre is the sun god, Tonatiuh. He is surrounded by symbols of the five world creations. The stone also shows the symbols of the 20 days of the solar month.**

**◀ This statue is of Coatlicue, the goddess of the earth.**

## Important gods

**HUITZILOPOCHTLI** was the god of war and the protector of the Aztecs. The Aztecs fought a special war, called The War of the Flowers, to capture victims to sacrifice to him.

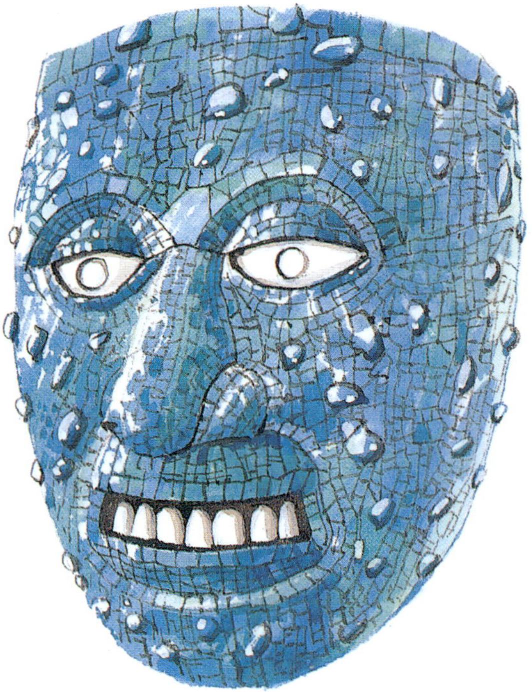

▲ **A mask of Quetzalcoatl.**

**QUETZALCOATL** was the god of learning and the arts. His name means *feathered serpent*. The original Quetzalcoatl was probably a leader of the Toltec people, who ruled ancient Mexico long before the Aztecs. According to Aztec legend, one day Quetzalcoatl would return to decide the fate of the Aztecs.

# Temples

The Aztecs built large **pyramids** to worship their gods. At the top of each one was a shrine where ceremonies took place and sacrifices were made.

Priests were highly thought of by the Aztecs. They studied the stars and tried to predict the future. Priests were the only people who went out after dark – everybody else was scared of evil spirits.

Near the temples were **tlachtli** courts where the sacred ball game, ulama, was played.

**DISK LINK**
**Fancy a go at the sacred ball game? Then take the TLACHTLI CHALLENGE!**

▲ The Aztecs performed thousands of human sacrifices every year.

◀ The Aztec pyramids had many steps, leading up to a shrine to the gods.

▼ Sharp, stone knives, such as this one, were used in the sacrifices.

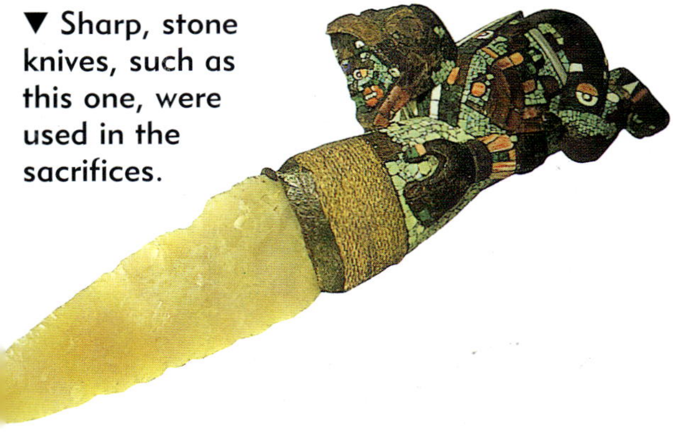

## Sacrifices

Human sacrifices were an important part of Aztec religion. The Aztecs believed that human hearts and blood kept their gods strong and powerful, and that the gods would protect the people and make their crops grow. The Aztecs also believed that if a brave soldier was sacrificed, his strength would be passed on to other warriors. At some ceremonies, Aztec people were sacrificed but most of the victims were prisoners of war.

Every morning, people made a small sacrifice by pricking their finger or ear lobe with a cactus needle and letting a drop of blood fall to the ground.

# Farming

Farming was essential to the Aztec way of life. Corn was the most important crop but the Aztecs also grew avocados, beans, chilli peppers and tomatoes. Each farmer gave the Great Speaker some of his crops to be stored away in case there was a famine.

There were two types of farmland. Some Aztec farmers cleared a small part of the land or forest by burning the vegetation. They would then plant crops in the fertile ashes. After a few years, when the land became less fertile, they would clear another area.

Around Tenochtitlan, the Aztecs dug up fertile mud from the lake bottom and heaped it on top of woven plant material to make little islands. The islands were called **chinampas**, or *floating gardens*.

**▶ Sometimes, trees were planted to anchor the chinampas to the bottom of the lake.**

**▼ A simple digging stick was used to prepare the land for planting crops.**

**DISK LINK**
Check out the chinampas when you take a ride in the AZTEC EXPLORER.

## Aztec crops

# Food

Meat was not a large part of the Aztecs' diet. There were few large animals to hunt and the Aztecs did not raise cattle or sheep. They ate lots of vegetables, such as corn, beans and peppers. A corn pancake, called a **tlaxcalli**, was eaten with most meals.

**DISK LINK**
**Feast your eyes on an Aztec marketplace in FOR SALE.**

## Food facts

● A chocolate drink was made from **cacao** beans. It was considered a luxury because cacao beans were also used as money!

● An alcoholic drink, called **pulque**, was made from a type of cactus.

● The Aztecs ate fish, turkeys, wild rabbits and even dogs.

**▼ The Aztecs served their food in pottery bowls and often ate using their fingers.**

## Make your own tlaxcallis

**Ingredients:**
2 cups flour
1 tsp salt
2 tbsp margarine
175 ml cold water

**1.** Mix the dry ingredients together. Then mix in the margarine until the mixture resembles bread crumbs.

**2.** Gradually add the water and stir it in with a wooden spoon until the mixture forms a stiff dough.

**3.** Divide the dough into 12 balls. On a floured surface, roll the balls out into flat, thin circles.

**4.** Ask an adult to help you fry them in a little oil for one minute on each side.

Serve your tlaxcallis warm. Fill them with chilli, avocado, beans, tomato and lettuce and roll them up!

# At home

Most Aztecs lived in small, one-room houses. They were made from mud and the roofs were thatched. Only wealthy people could afford large houses. They were often built on raised platforms and had walls made of stone. The walls were covered in limestone, which made the outside of the house white and shiny. They had several rooms that opened on to an inner courtyard.

Instead of a bathroom, many houses had a separate sweat room. This was made from stone and was heated by fires built around the outside walls. Inside, the people splashed water onto the hot walls to make them steam. They would stay inside until they began to sweat and then they would dash out and plunge into the nearest stream or pool.

**◀ A statue of the fire god, Xiuhtectuhtli, was placed in the hearth of every house.**

**▶ Aztec rooms, such as this one, had little furniture. The Aztecs sat on straw cushions and slept on mats in the corners of the room. Each house had a fireplace, where all the cooking was done. It was also used as a shrine to Xiuhtectuhtli, the fire god.**

**DISK LINK**
What were Aztec families like? What did people do in their spare time? Just ask THE GREAT SPEAKER!

# Language

The Aztecs spoke a language called Nahuatl. Instead of writing words made up of letters, they drew **pictograms**. These are pictures that stand for ideas or things. They were often joined together to form sentences, and were used to write down stories or as a way of keeping records. Aztec manuscripts, called **codices**, were made of folded deerskin or bark paper.

**▼ Many Aztec children went to schools that were run by their calpullis, or family groups. They were taught about religion, music and dancing. Boys also learned the skills that they needed to become warriors or tradesmen. Children from noble families went to a temple school, where boys were taught to become priests and girls learned to be temple assistants or midwives.**

**▲ The Aztecs played a variety of musical instruments, such as these flutes. Music was an important part of festivals and religious ceremonies.**

**▶ This Aztec codex shows offerings being made to the sun god at the top and the god of darkness at the bottom.**

## Common pictograms

Just like handwriting today, pictograms varied according to the person who drew them. Are any of these pictograms in the codex above?

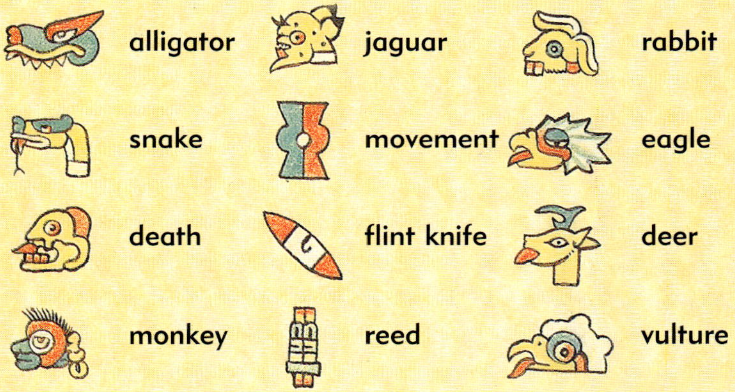

# Crafts

In Aztec times, a person's wealth was judged by the beauty of his possessions. A rich man could afford to have a skilled craftsman make the things he needed. Craftsmen were paid in food or other goods.

The Aztecs did not use metal for tools or weapons. They did not have iron or any other strong metal. Gold and copper were used to make delicate statues and jewellery.

**▲ Some Aztecs wore a golden ornament, such as this one, through their lips.**

The Aztecs made fine pots, decorated in gold. They did not have pottery wheels so they made pots by building up coils of clay and smoothing them out.

The volcanic rock found in Mexico is quite soft and it could easily be carved with the stone tools the Aztecs used. The people made detailed stone carvings and statues from stone.

Brightly coloured feathers were trimmed and bound together to make clothes and headdresses. They were also used to decorate warriors' shields and weapons.

**▼ This shield was made from feathers.**

A type of volcanic glass, called **obsidian**, was used to make vases, mirrors and blades for knives.

**▼ Mirrors, such as this one, were made from polished obsidian.**

# Clothes

Aztec clothes reflected a person's age and position in society. Most clothes were made from the fibre of a cactus, called the **maguey** plant. Only the rich could afford to wear cotton. Their garments were also brightly coloured and covered in beautiful embroidery. Warriors wore ornate feather headdresses and the most important soldiers were allowed to wear costumes that made them look like jaguars or eagles. Men wore a loincloth, called a **maxtlatl**, with a cape over one shoulder. Women wore skirts tied with a belt and a loose tunic on top.

Both men and women wore emerald, jade and opal jewellery. They also wore lots of bright, multicoloured make-up.

**DISK LINK**
**Stay on the lookout for clues that will help you through the SURVIVAL ADVENTURE.**

# Invasion!

Aztec civilisation was at its peak when Montezuma II was Great Speaker. At this time, far away in Europe, the Spanish were looking for new lands to conquer. In 1519, a Spaniard named Hernando Cortés arrived in Mexico with a crew of about 300 soldiers.

At first, the Aztecs believed that Cortés was the god Quetzalcoatl, returning to decide their fate as the priests had foretold. They did not know whether to welcome him or be wary of him.

Within two years, the Spanish had killed most of the Aztec people and destroyed the city of Tenochtitlan. The Aztecs were no match against the Spanish with their cannons and armour.

**▼ Aztec myths predicted that when Quetzalcoatl returned, he would have a pale face and a dark beard. To the Aztecs, Cortés looked just like the god, with his pale skin and dark beard.**

**DISK LINK**
**Step back in time to find out more about the Spanish invasion in TIME WARP.**

# Food for the people

**The Aztecs told many stories about their gods and about the world around them. Often these stories would attempt to explain something that the people did not really understand. This is the story of the discovery of corn.**

The gods found that creating people was much more difficult than creating the rest of the world! They had attempted to make people lots of times but each attempt had failed. Finally, they created some creatures that seemed to be just about right. There was only one problem. The people that they had made did not seem to know what to eat, or even how to eat. The people were starving but the gods couldn't figure out what to do about it. All the other animals they had created knew exactly how to feed themselves without any help.

The gods worried as they watched the people growing thinner. Every day, they tried to think of different ways to help the people find the food that they needed.

One day, some ants came to the place where the gods were discussing what to do about the starving people.

"We know where there is food," said one of the ants. "We will carry it here for you to give to the new people."

"Great!" said Quetzalcoatl, the god who was most worried about the people. "But why don't you just tell us where the food is and we will tell the people?"

"No, no, no!" said the ants. "We can't possibly do that. It's our secret."

The ants wanted the gods to look favourably upon them. They also thought that the people might be useful to them in the future. This is why they wanted the gods to rely on them to supply the people with food.

The next day, the ants carried food to the gods. This food was very small and hard. In fact, the pieces of it were so tiny that each of the ants could easily carry one grain. The gods had never seen anything like it! They chewed the hard grains until they were soft and then they placed them on the lips of the people. The people swallowed the grains and soon began to look and feel much better.

The ants continued to carry the food to the gods every day but they would not tell them where it came from. The gods had to wait patiently for the ants to bring the grains, then they would chew it for the people and place it on their lips.

As much as Quetzalcoatl loved the people, he became tired of feeding them. All the gods were falling behind in their responsibilities. While they were chewing the food for the people, they could not concentrate on making the Sun shine, or the rain fall, or the rivers flow. Each day, when the ants arrived with the grains, the gods sighed deeply and grew more and more irritated.

One day, Quetzalcoatl decided to find out where the food was for himself. He turned himself into a black ant and sat waiting for the ants to pass by. As the ants marched past, he slipped into line and marched with them. The procession led to the foot of a huge mountain then disappeared through a tiny crack in the rock. Inside the mountain there was an enormous cavern and Quetzalcoatl saw a huge pile of food. Copying the other ants, he picked up a grain and stepped back into the line.

When the procession of ants reached the gods, Quetzalcoatl returned to his own form. "You could not keep the secret of the food from me!" he said to the ants.

"But you need us to help you!" said one of the ants. "The people are much too big to fit in through the tiny crack in the side of the mountain."

Quetzalcoatl turned to the thunder god, and whispered in his ear. The thunder god stood up and raised his hand. All of the ants scuttled away in fear for their lives.

A flash of lightning struck the mountain, causing a huge crack and the grains of food spilt out over the ground. The people ran to see what had happened.

One of the people picked up a grain and put it in his mouth. The others copied him and ate their fill of food.

But there were many grains left over. Quetzalcoatl showed the people how to plant the grains so that more food would grow on new plants. These plants grew into the food we now call corn.

The gods were happy to know that the people could feed themselves. And the people were happy because they now knew what to eat and how to grow it.

As for the ants, they found that the people could still be useful. The people began to find other new and delicious foods that the ants could also share!

# How we know

How do we know about the Aztecs when they lived such a long time ago?

## Evidence from the ground

The Spanish invaders demolished most of Tenochtitlan, destroying a lot of the evidence of the Aztec way of life. However, some Aztec artefacts remain and the ruins of a few temples that were not destroyed are still standing today.

▲ **This temple was built in around AD 250, at Teotihuacan, in the Valley of Mexico. It is one of the few temples that has remained standing until today.**

▲ **Some Aztec codices have survived.**

## Evidence from books

The Spanish destroyed most of the Aztecs' codices, although a few have survived. One Spaniard, Bernardino de Sahagun, translated some Aztec codices soon after the conquest. Other members of the Spanish invading forces wrote accounts of Aztec life as it was when they arrived.

## Evidence around us

Today, descendants of the Aztecs still live in Mexico and some of their customs date back to Aztec times. Many speak a form of the Aztec language, Nahuatl, and some of the words have passed into other languages, such as *tomatl* (tomato), *chocolatl* (chocolate) and *ahuacatl* (avocado).

# Glossary

**Anahuac** The name that the Aztecs gave to the lands of their Empire in Mexico.

**cacao** A bean used to make chocolate and cocoa.

**calpulli** A group made up of closely related Aztec people. Each calpulli had a head man who made decisions for the group.

**causeways** A type of road built to cross water.

**chinampas** Small, island farms built by the Aztecs.

**codices** A type of ancient manuscript. Aztec codices were written on deerskin or bark paper and folded to make a book.

**digging stick** A simple, long, straight stick used to dig and plough the earth.

**empire** A large area of conquered lands, including many different towns.

**Great Speaker** The leader of the Aztec Empire. He was a brave warrior and a priest.

**maguey** A plant belonging to the cactus family.

**maxtlatl** A cloth wrapped and tied around the hips, worn by Aztec men.

**myths** Traditional stories about gods or heroes. Myths are sometimes based on the truth and they explain how people think about the world.

**obsidian** A type of glass that has a reflective surface.

**pictogram** A symbol that represents a thing, an idea or a word.

**plateau** A large area of high, flat land.

**pulque** An alcoholic drink made from the sap of the maguey plant.

**pyramids** Buildings with a square base and sloping sides. The Aztecs built pyramids as temples to worship their gods.

**sacrifice** Killing an animal or a person as an offering to the gods.

**tlachtli** The court where the sacred Aztec ball game, ulama, was played. Two opposing teams tried to pass a ball through a hoop using their elbows, hips and knees.

**tlaxcalli** An Aztec word for flat, corn pancakes. They are still eaten today but they are usually known by the Spanish word *tortilla*.

**tribute** A form of tax, paid to the Aztec ruler by the people living in the towns throughout the Aztec Empire.

# Work book

**Photocopy this sheet and use it to make your own notes.**

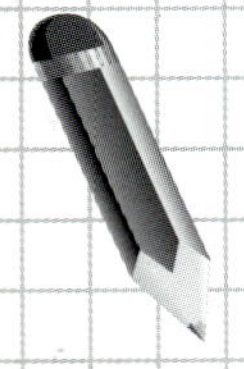

# Play patolli

Patolli was one of the Aztecs' favourite games and now you can play it on your disk. The rules are easy to learn. It is a two-player game, so you'll need someone to play against.

- Each player starts off with 10 jade pebbles and six counters. The idea of the game is to get your counters around the board and to win all of your opponent's pebbles.
- Before the game begins, both players must agree how many pebbles they are going to gamble. You must each bet the same number of pebbles.
- Players take turns to throw five cacoa beans. Each bean has a dot on it.
- If one dot lands face up, you can move one square or move a counter on to the board for the first time
- If two dots land face up, you can move two squares.
- If three dots land face up, you can move three squares.
- If four dots land face up, you can move four squares.
- But if five dots land face up, you can move TEN squares!

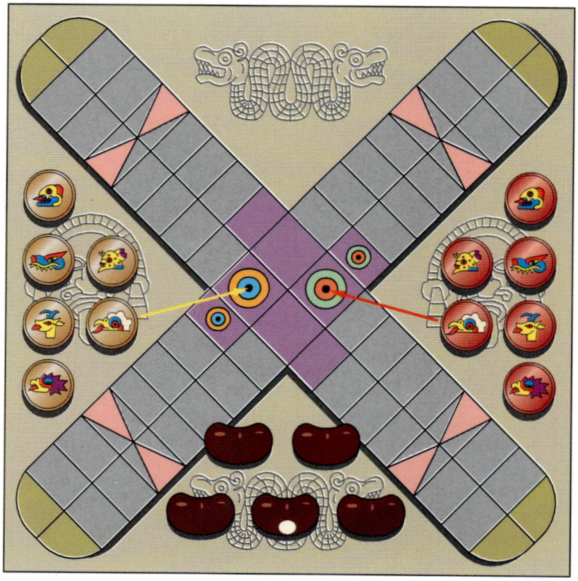

▲ The counters begin their journey around the board from the start squares. But before you can move a counter on to the board you must throw a one with the beans.

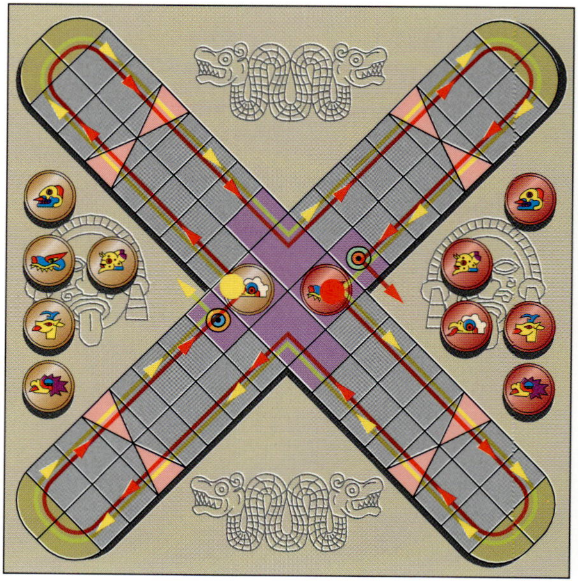

▲ The counters move in a clockwise direction until they reach the finish squares. Each player has their own finish square.

- When a counter lands on a finish square, it is taken off the board. Every time you get a counter off the board, your opponent must give you one of his jade pebbles.
- The first player to get all their counters off the board is the winner. The loser must now hand over the pebbles they bet at the beginning.
- If the loser still has some pebbles left the game starts again until someone wins all the pebbles.
- You must move one of your counters if you possibly can – you are not allowed to pass your go.
- You may only move one counter at a time – you are not allowed to split your throw between different counters.

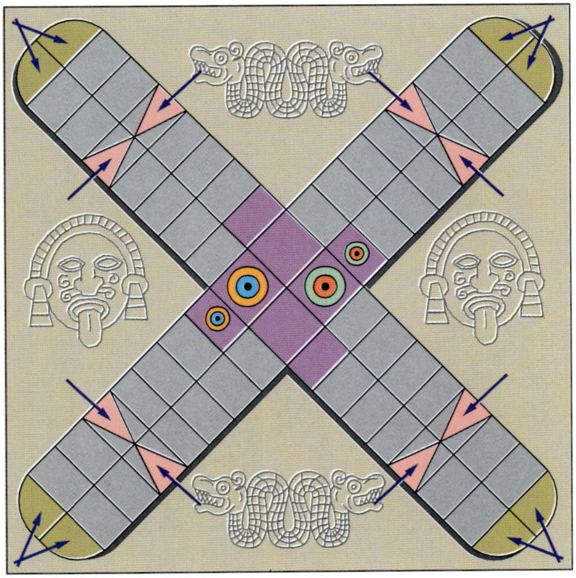

▲ Watch out for the eight squares marked with a triangle. If one of your counters land on one of these squares you must give your opponent two of your jade pebbles.

On the other hand, the two squares at each of the four ends of the board are good luck. Whenever one of your counters lands on one of these squares, you get another go and must throw the beans again. Hooray!

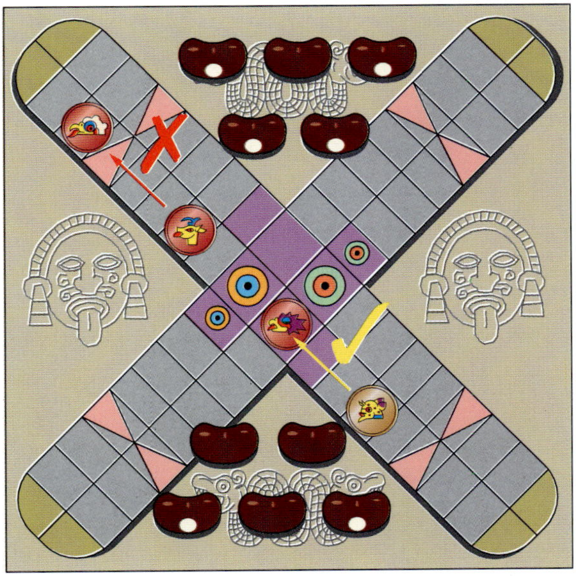

▲ You are not allowed to land on any square that is already occupied by one of your own pieces.

You are also not allowed on a square that is taken by one of your opponent's counters – unless it is on one of the eight purple squares in the middle of the board!

If you land on your opponent in one of these squares, their counter is taken off the board and must start all over again.

# Loading your INTERFACT disk

INTERFACT is available on floppy disk and CD-ROM for both PCs with Windows and Apple Macs. Make sure you follow the correct instructions for the disk you have chosen and your type of computer. Before you begin, check the minimum specification (inside front cover).

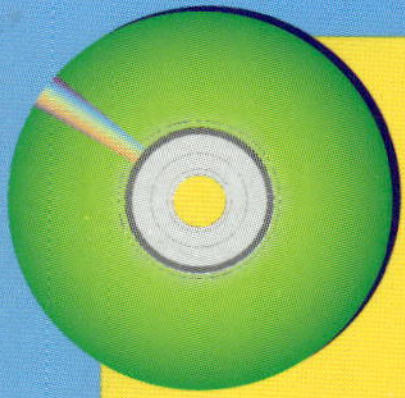

## CD-ROM INSTRUCTIONS

If you have a copy of INTERFACT on CD, you can run the program from the disk – you don't need to install it on your hard drive.

### PC WITH WINDOWS 95

1. Put the disk in the CD drive
2. Open MY COMPUTER
3. Double click on the CD drive icon
4. Double click on the icon called AZTECS

### PC WITH WINDOWS 3.1 OR 3.11

1. Put the disk in the CD drive
2. Select RUN from the FILE menu in the PROGRAM MANAGER
3. Type **D:\AZTECS** (Where D is the letter of your CD drive)
4. Press the RETURN key

### APPLE MAC

1. Put the disk in the CD drive
2. Double click on the INTERFACT icon
3. Double click on the icon called AZTECS

# FLOPPY DISK INSTRUCTIONS

If you have a copy of INTERFACT on floppy disk you must install the program on to your computer's hard drive before you can run it.

## PC WITH WINDOWS 3.1 OR 3.11

**To install INTERFACT:**

1. Put the disk in the floppy drive
2. Select RUN from the FILE menu in the PROGRAM MANAGER
3. Type **A:\INSTALL** (Where A is the letter of your floppy drive)
4. Click OK – unless you want to change the name of the INTERFACT directory

**To run INTERFACT:**

Once the program has installed, open the INTERFACT group in the PROGRAM MANAGER and double click on the icon called AZTECS

## PC WITH WINDOWS 95

**To install INTERFACT:**

1. Put the disk in the floppy drive
2. Select RUN from the START menu
3. Type **A:\INSTALL** (Where A is the letter of your floppy drive)
4. Click OK – unless you want to change the name of the INTERFACT directory

**To run INTERFACT:**

Once the program has installed, open the START menu and select PROGRAMS then select INTERFACT and click on the icon called AZTECS

## APPLE MAC

**To install INTERFACT:**

1. Put the disk in the floppy drive
2. Double click on the icon called INTERFACT INSTALLER
3. Click CONTINUE
4. Click INSTALL – unless you want to change the name of the INTERFACT folder

**To run INTERFACT:**

Once the program has installed, open the INTERFACT folder and double click on the icon called AZTECS

# How to use INTERFACT

INTERFACT is easy to use.
First find out how to load the program (see page 40) then read these simple instructions and dive in!

You will find that there are lots of different features to explore. Use the controls on the right-hand side of the screen to select the one you want to play. You will see that the main area of the screen changes as you click on to different features.

For example, this is what your screen will look like in For Sale, a scene from the ancient Aztec marketplace at Tlatelolco that you can explore. Once you've selected a feature, just click on the main screen to start playing.

Click here to select the feature you want to play.

Click on the arrow keys to scroll through the different features on the disk or find your way to the exit.

This is the reading box where instructions and directions appear explaining what to do. Go to page 4 to find out what's on the disk.

## DISK LINKS

When you read the book, you'll come across Disk Links. These show you where to find activities on the disk that relate to the page you are reading. Use the arrow keys to find the icon on screen that matches the one in the Disk Link.

**DISK LINK**
Put your Aztec know-how to the test when you take the TLACHTLI CHALLENGE.

## BOOKMARKS

As you play the features on the disk, you'll bump into Bookmarks. These show you where to look in the book for more information about the topic on screen. Just turn to the page of the book shown in the Bookmark.

## WORK BOOK

On pages 36 and 37 you'll find note pages to photocopy and use again and again. Use them to write down your discoveries as you go through the book and the disk.

# HOT DISK TIPS

- After you have chosen the feature you want to play, remember to move the cursor from the icon to the main screen before clicking on the mouse again.
- If you don't know how to use one of the on-screen controls, simply touch it with your cursor. An explanation will pop up in the reading box!
- Keep a close eye on the cursor. When it changes from an arrow to a hand click your mouse and something will happen.
- Any words that appear on screen in blue and underlined are 'hot'. This means you can touch them with the cursor for more information.
- Explore the screen! There are secret hot spots and hidden surprises to find.

# Troubleshooting

If you have a problem with the INTERFACT disk, you should find the solution here. You can also call the helpline on 0171 684 4050. The lines are open from 10am to 5pm, Monday to Friday, and calls are charged at normal rates. But remember to get permission from the person who pays the bill before you use the phone.

**QUICK FIXES** Run through these general checkpoints before consulting COMMON PROBLEMS (see opposite page).

QUICK FIXES

## PC WITH WINDOWS 3.1 OR 3.11

**1** Check that you have the minimum specification: 386/33Mhz, VGA colour monitor, 4 Mb of RAM.

**2** Make sure you have typed in the correct instructions: a colon (:) not a semi-colon (;) and a back slash (\) not a forward slash (/). Also, do not use punctuation or put any spaces between letters.

**3** It is important that you do not have any other programs running. Before you start **INTERFACT**, hold down the Control key and press Escape. If you find that other programs are open, click on them with the mouse, then click the End Task key.

QUICK FIXES

## PC WITH WINDOWS 95

**1** Make sure you have typed in the correct instructions: a colon (:) not a semi-colon (;) and a back slash(\) not a forward slash (/). Also, do not use punctuation or put any spaces between letters.

**2** It is important that you do not have any other programs running. Before you start **INTERFACT**, look at the task bar. If you find that other programs are open, click on them with the right mouse button and select Close from the pop-up menu.

QUICK FIXES

**APPLE MAC**

**1** Make sure that you have the minimum specification: 68020 processor, 640x480 colour display, system 7.0 (or a later version) and 4 Mb of RAM.

**2** It is important that you do not have any other programs running. Before you start **INTERFACT**, click on the application menu in the top right-hand corner. Select each of the open applications and select Quit from the File menu.

# COMMON PROBLEMS

**Symptom:** Cannot load disk.
**Problem:** There is not enough space available on your hard disk.
**Solution:** Make more space available by deleting old applications and programs you don't use until 6 Mb of free space is available.

**Symptom:** Disk will not run.
**Problem:** There is not enough memory available.
**Solution:** *Either* quit other applications and programs (see Quick Fixes) ***or*** increase your machine's RAM by adjusting the Virtual Memory.

**Symptom:** Graphics do not load or are of poor quality.
**Problem:** *Either* there is not enough memory available ***or*** you have the wrong display setting.
**Solution:** *Either* quit other applications and programs (see Quick Fixes) ***or*** make sure that your monitor control is set to 256 colours (MAC) or VGA (PC).

**Symptom:** There is no sound (PCs only).
**Problem:** Your sound card is not Soundblaster compatible.
**Solution:** Configure sound settings to make them Soundblaster compatible (see your sound card manual for more information).

**Symptom:** Your machine freezes.
**Problem:** There is not enough memory available.
**Solution:** *Either* quit other applications and programs (see Quick Fixes) ***or*** increase your machine's RAM by adjusting the Virtual Memory.

**Symptom:** Text does not fit neatly into boxes and 'hot' copy does not bring up extra information.
**Problem:** Standard fonts on your computer have been moved or deleted.
**Solution:** Re-install standard fonts. The PC version requires Arial; the Mac version requires Helvetica. See your computer manual for further information.

# Index

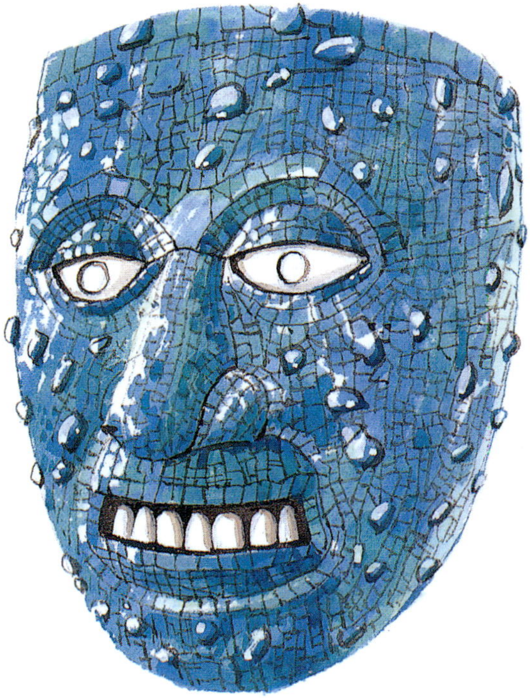